THIS COMPANION BELONGS TO

_____

Town&Country

Wine Companion

A TASTING GUIDE AND JOURNAL

TED LOOS

HEARST BOOKS

A division of Sterling Publishing Co., Inc.

New York / London
www.sterlingpublishing.com

Illustrator: Anne Smith
Project Editor: Catharine Wells
Designer: Barbara Balch

10 9 8 7 6 5 4 3 2 1

Published by Hearst Books
A Division of Sterling Publishing Co., Inc.
387 Park Avenue South, New York, NY 10016

Town & Country and Hearst Books are trademarks of
Hearst Communications, Inc.

www.townandcountrymag.com

For information about custom editions, special sales, premium
and corporate purchases, please contact Sterling Special Sales
Department at 800-805-5489 or specialsales@sterlingpub.com.

Distributed in Canada by Sterling Publishing
c/o Canadian Manda Group, 165 Dufferin Street
Toronto, Ontario, Canada M6K 3H6

Distributed in Australia by Capricorn Link (Australia) Pty. Ltd.
P.O. Box 704, Windsor, NSW 2756 Australia

Manufactured in China

Sterling ISBN 13: 978-158816-630-2
          ISBN 10: 1-58816-630-9

CONTENTS

 **FOREWORD**

WHAT IS IT ABOUT WINE that's so daunting? After all, it's no more than a potable liquid. Okay, not exactly. And, remember, even water—the world's *most* potable liquid—has gotten pretty complicated these days.

There are countless guides to wine available, many of them written by longtime connoisseurs who are at-the-ready to help budding oenophiles navigate their way through various vintages, a dizzying array of labels, the countries of origin, the varieties of grape and the most fertile regions on the map. The *Town & Country Wine Companion* is not one of them.

Rather, it is a clearly written primer to understanding the subtleties—and there are many—of wine in all its permutations. We begin with the basics: the ideal temperature for drinking wine. From there, we move on to its color (not merely a matter of red, white or rose), its aroma and, most importantly, its taste.

Developing a refined palate requires time and a fair amount of tasting (that's the fun part). To ease your way, we've provided a Tasting Journal, a handy glossary and a good number of inspiring quotes designed to lift your spirits (so to speak) as you lift your glass.

If you already have an extensive wine cellar, you probably don't need this book. But if you're a novice, eager to acquire an appreciation of wine and perhaps build a collection of your own, try starting here. If you do, you will find yourself in the fine company of author Ted Loos, whose main mission is to lead you to a glass of wine and not just to drink it, but to savor every sip.

—Pamela Fiori, Editor in Chief, *Town & Country*

# INTRODUCTION

IMAGINE THAT YOU'VE JUST MET SOMEONE at a cocktail party. The person seems charming. Would you immediately run off to Rio and elope?

Probably not. You're smarter than that. You would first get to know the person very well, and you'd think long and hard before accepting (or proposing) marriage, or even a trip to Rio.

Although not nearly as dangerous or as foolhardly as the Rio scenario, your approach to wine probably also qualifies as too fast, too soon.

It is only natural for you to open a bottle of wine at home and take a drink without even looking at it in the glass, or taking in its delicate "nose," as we call a wine's aromas. *Drinking* wine is easy and fun. You don't need a book to tell you that. *Tasting* wine takes a bit more effort—but it's ultimately far more rewarding. It requires you to slow down and take your time, something we're not really programmed to do in a world of Internet searches that take all of .00015 second.

The reason that most people say they can't remember a wine they've just tasted ten minutes ago is that they haven't tried very hard. This book proposes something just short of magic: to help you understand the complexities of wine just by closing your eyes and thinking hard. It sounds like something out of a children's fantasy book, but it's true.

Wine itself can seem magical, of course. A bunch of grapes, treated a certain way, become ambrosia, something to be savored and treasured. Every wine is different, and if it's good, it tells a story about where it came from.

We can't help giving wine some very human-sounding traits when we describe it: "deep," "cloying," "muscular," for example. It makes sense, since we're quite comfortable describing other people.

That's the reason we're calling this the *Town & Country Wine Companion*—it's not a notebook, a journal or a log. Wine can give you the companionship of a good friend, and so can this book.

GETTING STARTED

The correct wine temperature is crucial—most reds are served too warm and most whites too cold. Try taking whites *out* of the refrigerator fifteen minutes before serving, and unless reds have been in a classic cool cellar, put them in the refrigerator fifteen minutes before serving. Sixty to sixty-five degrees is appropriate for a red, and fifty to fifty-five degrees for a white. Champagne is served colder, around forty-five degrees.

We radically underuse our senses when we taste wine. To get all of them working together and to get the most out of the wine you've been looking forward to, the first rule is to eliminate all distractions.

One of the most important elements is a calm, serene space—you can't taste wine properly when your spouse is on the cell phone and distracting smells are wafting in from the kitchen and the kids have a DVD playing. I like jazz music on the CD player—Charles Mingus usually helps me focus—and no other activity or noise, but everyone has his or her own preference.

SEEING IS SAVORING

Probably the most underused wine-tasting sense is sight. You can tell a lot about a wine just from looking at it in the glass. A white tablecloth or napkin helps you see the wine's color against a neutral background. Color is the very first clue about what you'll be tasting. Wine of any color should be clear and brilliant, not cloudy or milky.

Once you've poured the wine into the glass—only one-third full, please, so that you can swirl it around in a minute—tip it gently forward with that white surface beneath it. You'll be able to get the full sense of its color, and then jot down some notes about it. When you're handling your wine glass, grab it by the stem every time. Holding the bowl of the glass in your hand heats the wine unnecessarily.

🍂 ENCHANTING AROMAS

Most people know they're supposed to smell a wine, but this isn't a quick sniff. Swirling the wine around a bit (in a way that doesn't get it on your clothes) helps aerate it, releasing the aromas and flavors.

Close your eyes and put your nose deep into the glass and inhale deeply. Then open your eyes, and think about what you just sensed. Then do it again. It may take several tries before you're ready to enter your impressions, but that's what this is all about—taking your time.

On the Palate

Given our approach so far, you won't be surprised to hear that once it comes to taste, you don't just drink the wine and call it a day. Sip some of the wine, but don't swallow it. Enjoy the experience of it in your mouth, and suck in a little air. Let it slosh around—all rules of polite imbibing are off the table when you're tasting wine. (You finally have a good excuse to ignore the rules your mother laid down about table manners.)

There's one cardinal rule when it comes to wine: The longer the pleasant, lingering taste of a wine lasts in your mouth once it's gone, the better the wine is. It's called the "finish," what would in another context be called the aftertaste. Wines with a short finish aren't necessarily bad, but they're not great, and they're never candidates for aging.

Be a Recording Artist

After each of these steps, you'll want to note your thoughts in the Tasting Journal. One of the best ways to learn about wine is to taste the same wine more than once, on different

days. Your impressions may vary slightly, and it will deepen your understanding of the wine. Another trick is to taste "flights" of similar wines. You learn a lot more about a single Napa Cabernet when you taste five of the same type alongside each other. You start to see commonalities among the regions or grapes, and places where they diverge.

Don't worry that you're still tentative after your first attempts to really taste wine. The more you do this, the better you get at it. Filling in entries in the companion will probably spur you to ask more questions of sommeliers in restaurants, to read up on wine in magazines and online and to begin more of a substantial dialogue with your local wine-shop proprietor. Perhaps you'll be inspired to take a wine-tasting course or visit some wineries. In other words, you'll further your wine education easily, and it won't seem like work.

Ultimately this companion is about helping you trust your own taste. If you like it, it's a good wine. That rule holds true no matter what—you don't have to give up the preferences you've developed over the years. Now you can begin to figure out exactly *why* you like a certain wine, and to act on those opinions. It's a breakthrough that will change the way you think about wine. And, the way you drink wine!

$\mathscr{C}$HAMPAGNE

PEOPLE TEND TO THROW AWAY their critical faculties when it comes to Champagne. It's often served in celebratory situations, so people aren't thinking, they're drinking. But Champagne is a wine, and all the same guidelines for tasting it apply.

Champagne is made from three grapes: Chardonnay, Pinot Noir and Pinot Meunier. (Don't forget that white wine can be made from red grapes simply by fermenting it without the skins, which is where the color lies.) They are often blended together, but some wines are 100 percent of one grape, and the label doesn't always reveal what's inside. When you're starting out, stick to wines that say "brut" on the label. This means dry, and most Champagnes fall into this category.

If you don't see a year on the label, it's called "non vintage" and was blended with grapes from different years. That's the most common way to make Champagne. Vintage Champagnes, from a single year, tend to be higher end and more expensive. For example, Krug's fabulous Salon de

SPARKLING WINES

CHAMPAGNE, from the Champagne region of France, is the most famous sparkling wine by far. But it's hardly the only one:

CAVA—This sparkler made in Northern Spain is earthy and tasty, and should be drunk young. Segura Viudas is a name to look for.

PROSECCO—This white grape from Italy's Veneto region is made into a wonderful sparkling wine that tastes of tart apples. Mionetto makes some good ones.

CALIFORNIA—A handful of good California wineries like Schramsberg use the traditional *méthode Champenoise* to craft elegant sparkling wines.

Mesnil is a wine that comes from just one vineyard and is always vintage bottled.

Bubbles are what make Champagne unique, of course. And they are also a crucial visual clue. Lots of fine, vigorous bubbles is a really good sign. Slow, fat bubbles—or the absence of bubbles—is a bad sign. The color of Champagne, like a white wine, can range from a pale straw to a deep golden hue. As Champagnes age—and they can age wonderfully—they tend to get a darker color.

When you're getting a sense of the wine's nose, watch out for inhaling too deeply—those bubbles are tiny explosions of carbon dioxide, and it may be a rude awakening to get too many at once. The nose of a Champagne comes out to meet you; it doesn't require your diving in.

Chardonnay-based wines will taste of apple, butter and nuts. Pinot Noir, a red grape, imparts the taste of what we call "red fruits"—strawberry, cherry and raspberry. (Rosé Champagne is made from Pinot Noir: The wine comes into contact with the red grape skins, producing that gorgeous pink color.)

The words "toasty" or "bready" frequently come up, especially in tasting older sparkling wines. In tasting Taittinger Comtes de Champagne rosé 1996 for *Town & Country*, I wrote that it had the flavors of a toasted brioche slice with plum jam—that gives you an idea of the richness and variety of tastes than can explode when you pop a Champagne cork.

CHAPTER 2

WHITE WINES

FOR SOME REASON, PEOPLE THINK that white wine, since it's translucent and seemingly less weighty, is less worthy of attention than red when it comes to tasting. Not so—heft and substance can lurk within that placid glass of bright liquid. And "white" doesn't do justice to the incredible array of colors that you can find, from a light hay color with a greenish cast to a rich bronze.

As white wines age, they tend to attain deeper color. Another color factor is aging in oak barrels: Wines that get this treatment have a more intense yellow. (Some grape varieties, like Chardonnay, simply make deeper-colored wine.) In any case, wine should look brilliant and enticing when you tip it back to examine it.

WHITE WINES

Here are some of the world's most important white grapes and what you can expect when you sample them with your senses:

CHARDONNAY—The king of white wines, known for its aromas of apple, butter and lemon, is made around the world and is the only grape allowed in white Burgundy. To see the heights it can hit, try a Montrachet Marquis de Laguiche from Maison Joseph Drouhin in Burgundy, France.

SAUVIGNON BLANC—Crisp and grassy, this wonderful grape has hit it big Down Under, among other places. Cloudy Bay in New Zealand makes a terrific example of this generally pale-colored wine.

RIESLING—Germany's best grape is known for being spicy, peachy and floral. It has powerful floral aromatics that you'll smell right away. German producer Robert Weil has mastered this fascinating grape.

PINOT GRIGIO—Also known as Pinot Gris in France and the United States. Italians swear by its tart, dry and seductive character, and you will too if you try the one made by Russiz Superiore in Italy's Friuli region.

Once you are ready to smell and taste, keep in mind what we might call the Rule of Fruit: The magic of grapes transforming gives every good wine—white or red or bubbly—the aroma of some kind of fruit. If you can discern only the oak used to age it, or just the prickly sensation of acid, it could be a lesser wine.

Typical white-wine fruit flavors include apple, pear, apricot and peach. But don't let that constrain your imagination. Gewürztraminers are known for tasting like lychee, and Sauvignon Blanc often reveals a grapefruit character.

It doesn't stop at fruit—flowers, grass, minerals and even gasoline are all legitimate tasting notes for a white wine. Close your eyes and get serious about writing down what you think, no matter how silly you think it sounds. You may find your fellow tasters are getting the same thing.

Acidity is the most important texture factor for a white wine, since by definition it lacks tannin, the stuff in a red that coats your teeth. Some grapes produce higher-acid wines—Austria's Grüner Veltliner, for instance.

Even whites that are bursting with sweet fruit aromas should have a good acid structure, which you'll notice as a tingle in the sides of your mouth. Think of it as the frame around the picture of the wine's flavors. Balance is the crucial factor. The wine's acid should be perfectly in balance with the rest of its personality.

Some white wines have some sugar left over from the fermentation process—winemaking is simply the conversion of natural sugars into alcohol. Don't be afraid of some sweetness, even in a non-dessert wine. As long as the sweetness is balanced by acidity, the wine has an interesting story to tell. Sweetness is generally the first thing you'll notice in a wine; then the other flavors and textures will come into play.

So how was the finish? Did it last and make you think, or did it fade away quickly? Don't rush into the next wine. Give the white you've just tasted some time to open up and reveal its true colors.

CHAPTER 3

RED WINES

FOR MANY PEOPLE, A GLASS of purplish-black, opaque liquid symbolizes the impenetrable mysteries of wine. How can they ever expect to understand something so dark and brooding? It's not as hard as it seems.

First things first: Red wine differs from white in that it is made from red grapes and then fermented with the skins on, giving it tannin and color. So it has extra elements of complexity to add to the ones we've already identified in white, like acidity and fruit.

The appearance of red wine is enormously important. Young and fruity wines tend to fall in the violet-to-ruby spectrum. Older wines often get a brick-colored cast, and like white wine, they tend toward brown as they age.

Red wine can sometimes produce sediment as it gets older, and this is normal. Decanting the wine can take care of that, and it can also help bring out the wine's flavors.

RED   WINES

Here are some of the world's most important red varietals and a few clues about what to look for:

CABERNET SAUVIGNON—For many wine lovers, Cab is king. It's usually the most important grape in red Bordeaux (often blended with Merlot and others), and it also rules in Napa Valley. Black cherry, cassis, mint and herbal are classic descriptions of its aroma. Napa's Caymus Vineyards makes an impeccable Cab.

SYRAH—Though native to France's Rhone Valley, Syrah is planted around the world, notably in Australia as Shiraz. Generally tannic and age-worthy, it tastes of blackberries, pepper, smoke and even a hint of bacon fat. If you want to be wowed by this dark-colored wine type, try Henschke's Hill of Grace from Down Under.

Even a young red wine with no sediment can benefit from decanting, because it's exposed to air—the same principle that leads us to swirl the wine in our glass. So try decanting

PINOT NOIR—Known for its strawberry-cherry flavors, age gives Pinot Noir an unusual complexity, including an earthy mushroom character. California's Santa Barbara County and Oregon's Willamette Valley are two American Pinot hubs. For the ultimate Pinot experience, open a single-vineyard red bottling from Burgundy's Domaine de la Romanée-Conti.

MERLOT—Softer in texture and with a rounder overall taste, Merlot is generally an easygoing grape. Plum, cherry and chocolate aromas abound. Washington State is home to some superb examples like Leonetti Cellar.

TEMPRANILLO—Spain's noblest red grape goes from strawberry and tea notes to earthy ones as it ages, and it's not usually very tannic—Pinot Noir fans should try it. It predominates in blends from Rioja, as in the fabulous wines of Finca Allende.

SANGIOVESE—This grape is at home in Tuscany—it's the foundation of Chianti—producing medium-colored red wines with a high acidity level that makes them easy to match with food. Marchesi de' Frescobaldi makes many great Sangiovese-based wines at all price levels.

any red wine for an hour before you taste it; it's also a great excuse to show off some beautiful crystal decanters.

Decanting is easy. Store the wine upright in the bottle for several hours, letting the sediment fall to the bottom. Then pour the wine slowly into a decanter, making sure that the sediment doesn't come along with the wine, especially right at the end of the process. If it happens to be a wine with a lot of sediment, decanting ensures that your tasting experience won't be a disaster before it's even started.

We're not done with appearance yet—the last big clue is that as reds age, you'll notice a distinct clear rim around the liquid in the glass. The bigger and more noticeable the rim, the older the wine.

Now, to the bouquet. Red wines will often lead you into a berry patch. Cherry, raspberry and strawberry are frequent descriptors you'll be using. Wines aged in oak will often taste of vanilla or toast. Some red wines like Pinot Noir will get a gamey or earthy smell—within reason, this is a good thing. In Cabernet Sauvignon or Cabernet Franc, herbal notes will often be in the mix. Mellow Merlot has been known to taste of chocolate.

Once you've taken in the bouquet and actually tasted the wine, see how the texture feels in your mouth. The presence of tannin will vary greatly—in a young Shiraz from Australia or a Barolo from Italy (made from the Nebbiolo grape) you may find your teeth and cheeks are immediately coated, but in some older wines it will be barely noticeable. As wines age, the tannins soften, becoming "rounder."

The important thing, as always, is that the tannin be in balance with the wine's other elements. No one taste or texture element should dominate. The harmonious whole is what counts.

TASTING JOURNAL

A WINE'S LABEL GIVES YOU lots of important information, but don't get too hung up on grape varieties. Some wines, like Barolo from Italy, are named for their region, not their component grapes, and many wines are blended from several varietals. If you can't find the information you want on a label, consider it an invitation to do a bit of online research to increase your knowledge.

Your first *Companion* entries may be extensive as you work to sort out what's relevant—that's good. You'll learn to streamline as you go, and your notes may be relevant later on for future tastings. Check the glossary in the back of the *Companion* for entries that may help you put words to your impressions.

Remember, there are no bad grapes—great wine can come from any of them in the hands of the right producer.

Here's a sample entry, a wine I recently tasted and loved, to get you started.

DATE: *5 / 27 / 06*

OCCASION: *Dinner party*

LOCATION: *The Sherwin-Andersons*

WINE NAME: *Chateau Palmer*

PRODUCER: *Palmer*

GRAPE VARIETIES: *Not listed, but Cabernet Sauvignon, Merlot, and Petit Verdot are likely for red Bordeaux.*

VINTAGE: *1970*

REGION: *Bordeaux*

SUB REGION OR SINGLE VINEYARD (WHERE APPROPRIATE): *Margaux*

OTHER NOTABLE BOTTLE INFORMATION: *None*

APPEARANCE: *Quite dark and plum-colored, with very little clear rim, indicating age—unusually youthful-looking for a 36-year-old wine. Slight* *cloudiness due to sediment, but nothing to worry about.*

A R O M A : *We decanted it for 20 minutes but it was fairly "dumb" at the start—it was not revealing itself much. My friend Michael, who brought it, called it a "tight, berry nose" and that seems right. Cedar and cassis aromas were present but there was no real hint of development as you'd expect in a wine of this age.*

T A S T E : *This tastes almost like a tannic, young wine. It has a nice grip, but the tannins are round and sophisticated. It took quite some time for it to reveal a lot of flavors on the palate. Nice black currant edge but still a bit clenched—it needs five to ten years to develop properly. A hint of brown sugar was present.*

O V E R A L L I M P R E S S I O N S : *A very happy surprise, a wine that can be drunk in 10 years or more down the road.*

____ UNIMPRESSIVE

____ GOOD FOR EVERYDAY

_X_ SPECIAL OCCASION

GOD MADE ONLY WATER,
BUT MAN MADE WINE.—Victor Hugo

DATE:

OCCASION:

LOCATION:

WINE NAME:

PRODUCER:

GRAPE VARIETIES:

VINTAGE:

REGION:

SUB REGION OR SINGLE VINEYARD
(WHERE APPROPRIATE):

OTHER NOTABLE BOTTLE INFORMATION:

APPEARANCE:

AROMA:

TASTE:

OVERALL IMPRESSIONS:

_____ UNIMPRESSIVE

_____ GOOD FOR EVERYDAY

_____ SPECIAL OCCASION

🍇 **THE BEST USE OF BAD WINE IS TO DRIVE AWAY POOR RELATIONS.** —French proverb

DATE:

OCCASION:

LOCATION:

WINE NAME:

PRODUCER:

GRAPE VARIETIES:

VINTAGE:

REGION:

SUB REGION OR SINGLE VINEYARD (WHERE APPROPRIATE):

OTHER NOTABLE BOTTLE INFORMATION:

APPEARANCE:

AROMA:

TASTE:

OVERALL IMPRESSIONS:

_____ UNIMPRESSIVE

_____ GOOD FOR EVERYDAY

_____ SPECIAL OCCASION

QUICKLY BRING ME A BEAKER OF WINE, SO THAT I MAY WET MY MIND AND SAY SOMETHING CLEVER.—Aristophanes

DATE:

OCCASION:

LOCATION:

WINE NAME:

PRODUCER:

GRAPE VARIETIES:

VINTAGE:

REGION:

SUB REGION OR SINGLE VINEYARD
(WHERE APPROPRIATE):

OTHER NOTABLE BOTTLE INFORMATION:

APPEARANCE:

_____

_____

_____

AROMA:

_____

_____

_____

TASTE:

_____

_____

_____

OVERALL IMPRESSIONS:

_____

_____

_____

_____

🍁 ____ UNIMPRESSIVE

🍁 🍁 ____ GOOD FOR EVERYDAY

🍁 🍁 🍁 ____ SPECIAL OCCASION

GIVE ME WINE TO WASH ME CLEAN OF THE WEATHER-STAINS OF CARE.—Ralph Waldo Emerson

DATE:

OCCASION:

LOCATION:

WINE NAME:

PRODUCER:

GRAPE VARIETIES:

VINTAGE:

REGION:

SUB REGION OR SINGLE VINEYARD
(WHERE APPROPRIATE):

OTHER NOTABLE BOTTLE INFORMATION:

APPEARANCE:

AROMA:

TASTE:

OVERALL IMPRESSIONS:

_____ UNIMPRESSIVE

_____ GOOD FOR EVERYDAY

_____ SPECIAL OCCASION

MY ONLY REGRET IN LIFE IS THAT I DID NOT DRINK MORE CHAMPAGNE.—John Maynard Keynes

DATE:

OCCASION:

LOCATION:

WINE NAME:

PRODUCER:

GRAPE VARIETIES:

VINTAGE:

REGION:

SUB REGION OR SINGLE VINEYARD (WHERE APPROPRIATE):

OTHER NOTABLE BOTTLE INFORMATION:

APPEARANCE:

AROMA:

TASTE:

OVERALL IMPRESSIONS:

_____ UNIMPRESSIVE

_____ GOOD FOR EVERYDAY

_____ SPECIAL OCCASION

WHEN THERE IS PLENTY OF WINE, SORROW AND WORRY TAKE WING.—Ovid

DATE:

OCCASION:

LOCATION:

WINE NAME:

PRODUCER:

GRAPE VARIETIES:

VINTAGE:

REGION:

SUB REGION OR SINGLE VINEYARD
(WHERE APPROPRIATE):

OTHER NOTABLE BOTTLE INFORMATION:

APPEARANCE:

AROMA:

TASTE:

OVERALL IMPRESSIONS:

_____ UNIMPRESSIVE

_____ GOOD FOR EVERYDAY

_____ SPECIAL OCCASION

WINE, MADAM, IS GOD'S NEXT BEST GIFT TO MAN.—Ambrose Bierce

DATE:

OCCASION:

LOCATION:

WINE NAME:

PRODUCER:

GRAPE VARIETIES:

VINTAGE:

REGION:

SUB REGION OR SINGLE VINEYARD
(WHERE APPROPRIATE):

OTHER NOTABLE BOTTLE INFORMATION:

APPEARANCE:

AROMA:

TASTE:

OVERALL IMPRESSIONS:

____ UNIMPRESSIVE

____ GOOD FOR EVERYDAY

____ SPECIAL OCCASION

 **IN WINE THERE IS TRUTH.**—Pliny the Elder

DATE:

OCCASION:

LOCATION:

WINE NAME:

PRODUCER:

GRAPE VARIETIES:

VINTAGE:

REGION:

**SUB REGION OR SINGLE VINEYARD
(WHERE APPROPRIATE):**

OTHER NOTABLE BOTTLE INFORMATION:

APPEARANCE:

AROMA:

TASTE:

OVERALL IMPRESSIONS:

_____ UNIMPRESSIVE

_____ GOOD FOR EVERYDAY

_____ SPECIAL OCCASION

WINE CAN OF THEIR WITS THE WISE BEGUILE, MAKE THE SAGE FROLIC, AND THE SERIOUS SMILE.

—Homer

DATE:

OCCASION:

LOCATION:

WINE NAME:

PRODUCER:

GRAPE VARIETIES:

VINTAGE:

REGION:

SUB REGION OR SINGLE VINEYARD (WHERE APPROPRIATE):

OTHER NOTABLE BOTTLE INFORMATION:

APPEARANCE:

AROMA:

TASTE:

OVERALL IMPRESSIONS:

____ UNIMPRESSIVE

____ GOOD FOR EVERYDAY

____ SPECIAL OCCASION

WINE MAKES DAILY LIVING EASIER, LESS HURRIED, WITH FEWER TENSIONS AND MORE TOLERANCE.—Benjamin Franklin

DATE:

OCCASION:

LOCATION:

WINE NAME:

PRODUCER:

GRAPE VARIETIES:

VINTAGE:

REGION:

SUB REGION OR SINGLE VINEYARD
(WHERE APPROPRIATE):

OTHER NOTABLE BOTTLE INFORMATION:

APPEARANCE:

AROMA:

TASTE:

OVERALL IMPRESSIONS:

🍂 ____ UNIMPRESSIVE

🍂 🍂 ____ GOOD FOR EVERYDAY

🍂 🍂 🍂 ____ SPECIAL OCCASION

WINE IS THE MOST CIVILIZED THING IN THE WORLD. —Ernest Hemingway

DATE:

OCCASION:

LOCATION:

WINE NAME:

PRODUCER:

GRAPE VARIETIES:

VINTAGE:

REGION:

SUB REGION OR SINGLE VINEYARD
(WHERE APPROPRIATE):

OTHER NOTABLE BOTTLE INFORMATION:

APPEARANCE:

AROMA:

TASTE:

OVERALL IMPRESSIONS:

____ UNIMPRESSIVE

____ GOOD FOR EVERYDAY

____ SPECIAL OCCASION

 HE WHO LOVES NOT WOMEN, WINE, AND SONG
REMAINS A FOOL HIS WHOLE LIFE LONG.

—Martin Luther

DATE:

OCCASION:

LOCATION:

WINE NAME:

PRODUCER:

GRAPE VARIETIES:

VINTAGE:

REGION:

SUB REGION OR SINGLE VINEYARD
(WHERE APPROPRIATE):

OTHER NOTABLE BOTTLE INFORMATION:

APPEARANCE:

AROMA:

TASTE:

OVERALL IMPRESSIONS:

_____ UNIMPRESSIVE

_____ GOOD FOR EVERYDAY

_____ SPECIAL OCCASION

THIS IS ONE OF THE DISADVANTAGES OF WINE. IT MAKES A MAN MISTAKE WORDS FOR THOUGHTS.—Samuel Johnson

DATE:

OCCASION:

LOCATION:

WINE NAME:

PRODUCER:

GRAPE VARIETIES:

VINTAGE:

REGION:

SUB REGION OR SINGLE VINEYARD
(WHERE APPROPRIATE):

OTHER NOTABLE BOTTLE INFORMATION:

APPEARANCE:

AROMA:

TASTE:

OVERALL IMPRESSIONS:

🍁 _____ UNIMPRESSIVE

🍁 🍁 _____ GOOD FOR EVERYDAY

🍁 🍁 🍁 _____ SPECIAL OCCASION

I NEVER UNDERSTOOD A SINGLE WORD HE SAID BUT I HELPED HIM DRINK HIS WINE... AND HE ALWAYS HAD SOME MIGHTY FINE WINE.

—Three Dog Night, "Joy to the World"

DATE:

OCCASION:

LOCATION:

WINE NAME:

PRODUCER:

GRAPE VARIETIES:

VINTAGE:

REGION:

SUB REGION OR SINGLE VINEYARD
(WHERE APPROPRIATE):

OTHER NOTABLE BOTTLE INFORMATION:

APPEARANCE:

AROMA:

TASTE:

OVERALL IMPRESSIONS:

____ UNIMPRESSIVE

____ GOOD FOR EVERYDAY

____ SPECIAL OCCASION

WE ARE ALL MORTAL UNTIL THE FIRST KISS
AND THE SECOND GLASS OF WINE.—Eduardo Galeano

DATE:

OCCASION:

LOCATION:

WINE NAME:

PRODUCER:

GRAPE VARIETIES:

VINTAGE:

REGION:

SUB REGION OR SINGLE VINEYARD
(WHERE APPROPRIATE):

OTHER NOTABLE BOTTLE INFORMATION:

APPEARANCE:

AROMA:

TASTE:

OVERALL IMPRESSIONS:

🍂 ____ UNIMPRESSIVE

🍂 🍂 ____ GOOD FOR EVERYDAY

🍂 🍂 🍂 ____ SPECIAL OCCASION

MARRIAGE IS LIKE WINE. IT IS NOT PROPERLY JUDGED UNTIL THE SECOND GLASS.—Douglas William Jerrold

DATE:

OCCASION:

LOCATION:

WINE NAME:

PRODUCER:

GRAPE VARIETIES:

VINTAGE:

REGION:

SUB REGION OR SINGLE VINEYARD
(WHERE APPROPRIATE):

OTHER NOTABLE BOTTLE INFORMATION:

APPEARANCE:

AROMA:

TASTE:

OVERALL IMPRESSIONS:

_____ UNIMPRESSIVE

_____ GOOD FOR EVERYDAY

_____ SPECIAL OCCASION

I FIND FRIENDSHIP TO BE LIKE WINE, RAW WHEN NEW, RIPENED WITH AGE, THE TRUE OLD MAN'S MILK AND RESTORATIVE CORDIAL.

—Thomas Jefferson

DATE:

OCCASION:

LOCATION:

WINE NAME:

PRODUCER:

GRAPE VARIETIES:

VINTAGE:

REGION:

SUB REGION OR SINGLE VINEYARD
(WHERE APPROPRIATE):

OTHER NOTABLE BOTTLE INFORMATION:

APPEARANCE:

AROMA:

TASTE:

OVERALL IMPRESSIONS:

_____ UNIMPRESSIVE

_____ GOOD FOR EVERYDAY

_____ SPECIAL OCCASION

WINE AND CHEESE ARE AGELESS COMPANIONS, LIKE ASPIRIN AND ACHES, OR JUNE AND MOON, OR GOOD PEOPLE AND NOBLE VENTURES.

—M.F.K. Fisher

DATE:

OCCASION:

LOCATION:

WINE NAME:

PRODUCER:

GRAPE VARIETIES:

VINTAGE:

REGION:

SUB REGION OR SINGLE VINEYARD
(WHERE APPROPRIATE):

OTHER NOTABLE BOTTLE INFORMATION:

APPEARANCE:

AROMA:

TASTE:

OVERALL IMPRESSIONS:

_____ UNIMPRESSIVE

_____ GOOD FOR EVERYDAY

_____ SPECIAL OCCASION

I DRINK CHAMPAGNE WHEN I'M HAPPY AND WHEN I'M SAD. SOMETIMES I DRINK IT WHEN I'M ALONE. WHEN I HAVE COMPANY I CONSIDER IT OBLIGATORY. I TRIFLE WITH IT IF I'M NOT HUNGRY AND DRINK IT WHEN I AM. OTHERWISE I NEVER TOUCH IT——UNLESS I'M THIRSTY.

—Madame Lilly Bollinger

DATE:

OCCASION:

LOCATION:

WINE NAME:

PRODUCER:

GRAPE VARIETIES:

VINTAGE:

REGION:

SUB REGION OR SINGLE VINEYARD
(WHERE APPROPRIATE):

OTHER NOTABLE BOTTLE INFORMATION:

APPEARANCE:

AROMA:

TASTE:

OVERALL IMPRESSIONS:

____ UNIMPRESSIVE

____ GOOD FOR EVERYDAY

____ SPECIAL OCCASION

 **WINE REJOICES THE HEART OF MAN,
AND JOY IS THE MOTHER OF ALL VIRTUES.**

—Johann Wolfgang von Goethe

DATE:

OCCASION:

LOCATION:

WINE NAME:

PRODUCER:

GRAPE VARIETIES:

VINTAGE:

REGION:

**SUB REGION OR SINGLE VINEYARD
(WHERE APPROPRIATE):**

OTHER NOTABLE BOTTLE INFORMATION:

APPEARANCE:

AROMA:

TASTE:

OVERALL IMPRESSIONS:

____ UNIMPRESSIVE

____ GOOD FOR EVERYDAY

____ SPECIAL OCCASION

MY DEAR GIRL, THERE ARE SOME THINGS THAT JUST AREN'T DONE, SUCH AS DRINKING DOM PÉRIGNON '53 ABOVE THE TEMPERATURE OF 38° FAHRENHEIT.—James Bond in Ian Fleming's *Goldfinger*

DATE:

OCCASION:

LOCATION:

WINE NAME:

PRODUCER:

GRAPE VARIETIES:

VINTAGE:

REGION:

SUB REGION OR SINGLE VINEYARD (WHERE APPROPRIATE):

OTHER NOTABLE BOTTLE INFORMATION:

APPEARANCE:

AROMA:

TASTE:

OVERALL IMPRESSIONS:

____ UNIMPRESSIVE

____ GOOD FOR EVERYDAY

____ SPECIAL OCCASION

A BOTTLE OF GOOD WINE, LIKE A GOOD ACT, SHINES EVER IN THE RETROSPECT.

—Robert Louis Stevenson

DATE:

OCCASION:

LOCATION:

WINE NAME:

PRODUCER:

GRAPE VARIETIES:

VINTAGE:

REGION:

SUB REGION OR SINGLE VINEYARD
(WHERE APPROPRIATE):

OTHER NOTABLE BOTTLE INFORMATION:

APPEARANCE:

AROMA:

TASTE:

OVERALL IMPRESSIONS:

____ UNIMPRESSIVE

____ GOOD FOR EVERYDAY

____ SPECIAL OCCASION

🍂 **WINE CHEERS THE SAD, REVIVES THE OLD, INSPIRES THE YOUNG, MAKES WEARINESS FORGET HIS TOIL.**—Lord Byron

DATE:

OCCASION:

LOCATION:

WINE NAME:

PRODUCER:

GRAPE VARIETIES:

VINTAGE:

REGION:

**SUB REGION OR SINGLE VINEYARD
(WHERE APPROPRIATE):**

OTHER NOTABLE BOTTLE INFORMATION:

APPEARANCE:

AROMA:

TASTE:

OVERALL IMPRESSIONS:

____ UNIMPRESSIVE

____ GOOD FOR EVERYDAY

____ SPECIAL OCCASION

I COOK WITH WINE; SOMETIMES I EVEN ADD IT TO THE FOOD.—W.C. Fields

DATE:

OCCASION:

LOCATION:

WINE NAME:

PRODUCER:

GRAPE VARIETIES:

VINTAGE:

REGION:

SUB REGION OR SINGLE VINEYARD
(WHERE APPROPRIATE):

OTHER NOTABLE BOTTLE INFORMATION:

APPEARANCE:

AROMA:

TASTE:

OVERALL IMPRESSIONS:

____ UNIMPRESSIVE

____ GOOD FOR EVERYDAY

____ SPECIAL OCCASION

WINE BRINGS TO LIGHT THE HIDDEN SECRETS OF THE SOUL, GIVES BEING TO OUR HOPES, BIDS THE COWARD FIGHT, DRIVES DULL CARE AWAY, AND TEACHES NEW MEANS FOR THE ACCOMPLISHMENT OF OUR WISHES.—Horace

DATE:

OCCASION:

LOCATION:

WINE NAME:

PRODUCER:

GRAPE VARIETIES:

VINTAGE:

REGION:

SUB REGION OR SINGLE VINEYARD (WHERE APPROPRIATE):

OTHER NOTABLE BOTTLE INFORMATION:

APPEARANCE:

AROMA:

TASTE:

OVERALL IMPRESSIONS:

🌿 ____ UNIMPRESSIVE

🌿 🌿 ____ GOOD FOR EVERYDAY

🌿 🌿 🌿 ____ SPECIAL OCCASION

ANYONE WHO TRIES TO MAKE YOU BELIEVE THAT HE KNOWS ALL ABOUT WINES IS OBVIOUSLY A FAKE.—Leon Adams

DATE:

OCCASION:

LOCATION:

WINE NAME:

PRODUCER:

GRAPE VARIETIES:

VINTAGE:

REGION:

SUB REGION OR SINGLE VINEYARD
(WHERE APPROPRIATE):

OTHER NOTABLE BOTTLE INFORMATION:

APPEARANCE:

AROMA:

TASTE:

OVERALL IMPRESSIONS:

_____ UNIMPRESSIVE

_____ GOOD FOR EVERYDAY

_____ SPECIAL OCCASION

WINE IS BOTTLED POETRY.

—Robert Louis Stevenson

DATE:

OCCASION:

LOCATION:

WINE NAME:

PRODUCER:

GRAPE VARIETIES:

VINTAGE:

REGION:

**SUB REGION OR SINGLE VINEYARD
(WHERE APPROPRIATE):**

OTHER NOTABLE BOTTLE INFORMATION:

APPEARANCE:

AROMA:

TASTE:

OVERALL IMPRESSIONS:

🍂 ____ UNIMPRESSIVE

🍂 🍂 ____ GOOD FOR EVERYDAY

🍂 🍂 🍂 ____ SPECIAL OCCASION

TO CLEAN GLASSES AND OLD CORKS.

DATE:

OCCASION:

LOCATION:

WINE NAME:

PRODUCER:

GRAPE VARIETIES:

VINTAGE:

REGION:

SUB REGION OR SINGLE VINEYARD
(WHERE APPROPRIATE):

OTHER NOTABLE BOTTLE INFORMATION:

APPEARANCE:

AROMA:

TASTE:

OVERALL IMPRESSIONS:

🍃 ____ UNIMPRESSIVE

🍃 🍃 ____ GOOD FOR EVERYDAY

🍃 🍃 🍃 ____ SPECIAL OCCASION

DRINK WINE, AND LIVE HERE BLITHEFUL WHILE YE MAY; THE MORROW'S LIFE TOO LATE IS——LIVE TODAY!

DATE:

OCCASION:

LOCATION:

WINE NAME:

PRODUCER:

GRAPE VARIETIES:

VINTAGE:

REGION:

SUB REGION OR SINGLE VINEYARD
(WHERE APPROPRIATE):

OTHER NOTABLE BOTTLE INFORMATION:

APPEARANCE:

AROMA:

TASTE:

OVERALL IMPRESSIONS:

🍁 ____ UNIMPRESSIVE

🍁 🍁 ____ GOOD FOR EVERYDAY

🍁 🍁 🍁 ____ SPECIAL OCCASION

🍂 **HERE'S TO WATER, WATER DIVINE—IT DEWS THE GRAPES THAT GIVE US WINE.**— Omar Khayyam

DATE:

OCCASION:

LOCATION:

WINE NAME:

PRODUCER:

GRAPE VARIETIES:

VINTAGE:

REGION:

SUB REGION OR SINGLE VINEYARD (WHERE APPROPRIATE):

OTHER NOTABLE BOTTLE INFORMATION:

APPEARANCE:

AROMA:

TASTE:

OVERALL IMPRESSIONS:

🍁 ____ UNIMPRESSIVE

🍁 🍁 ____ GOOD FOR EVERYDAY

🍁 🍁 🍁 ____ SPECIAL OCCASION

 **TO THE BIG-BELLIED BOTTLE.**

DATE:

OCCASION:

LOCATION:

WINE NAME:

PRODUCER:

GRAPE VARIETIES:

VINTAGE:

REGION:

SUB REGION OR SINGLE VINEYARD
(WHERE APPROPRIATE):

OTHER NOTABLE BOTTLE INFORMATION:

APPEARANCE:

AROMA:

TASTE:

OVERALL IMPRESSIONS:

_____ UNIMPRESSIVE

_____ GOOD FOR EVERYDAY

_____ SPECIAL OCCASION

WHEN WINE ENLIVENS THE HEART
MAY FRIENDSHIP SURROUND THE TABLE.

DATE:

OCCASION:

LOCATION:

WINE NAME:

PRODUCER:

GRAPE VARIETIES:

VINTAGE:

REGION:

SUB REGION OR SINGLE VINEYARD
(WHERE APPROPRIATE):

OTHER NOTABLE BOTTLE INFORMATION:

APPEARANCE:

AROMA:

TASTE:

OVERALL IMPRESSIONS:

🍁 ____ UNIMPRESSIVE

🍁 🍁 ____ GOOD FOR EVERYDAY

🍁 🍁 🍁 ____ SPECIAL OCCASION

🍇 WINE AND WOMEN——MAY WE ALWAYS HAVE A TASTE FOR BOTH.

DATE:

OCCASION:

LOCATION:

WINE NAME:

PRODUCER:

GRAPE VARIETIES:

VINTAGE:

REGION:

SUB REGION OR SINGLE VINEYARD
(WHERE APPROPRIATE):

OTHER NOTABLE BOTTLE INFORMATION:

APPEARANCE:

AROMA:

TASTE:

OVERALL IMPRESSIONS:

🍃 ____ UNIMPRESSIVE

🍃🍃 ____ GOOD FOR EVERYDAY

🍃🍃🍃 ____ SPECIAL OCCASION

ONE BARREL OF WINE CAN WORK MORE MIRACLES THAN A CHURCH FULL OF SAINTS.—Italian Proverb

DATE:

OCCASION:

LOCATION:

WINE NAME:

PRODUCER:

GRAPE VARIETIES:

VINTAGE:

REGION:

SUB REGION OR SINGLE VINEYARD
(WHERE APPROPRIATE):

OTHER NOTABLE BOTTLE INFORMATION:

APPEARANCE:

AROMA:

TASTE:

OVERALL IMPRESSIONS:

🍃 ____ UNIMPRESSIVE

🍃 🍃 ____ GOOD FOR EVERYDAY

🍃 🍃 🍃 ____ SPECIAL OCCASION

MAY FRIENDSHIP, LIKE WINE, IMPROVE AS TIME ADVANCES, AND MAY WE ALWAYS HAVE OLD WINE, OLD FRIENDS, AND YOUNG CARES.

DATE:

OCCASION:

LOCATION:

WINE NAME:

PRODUCER:

GRAPE VARIETIES:

VINTAGE:

REGION:

SUB REGION OR SINGLE VINEYARD (WHERE APPROPRIATE):

OTHER NOTABLE BOTTLE INFORMATION:

APPEARANCE:

AROMA:

TASTE:

OVERALL IMPRESSIONS:

____ UNIMPRESSIVE

____ GOOD FOR EVERYDAY

____ SPECIAL OCCASION

 **MAY YOUR LOVE BE LIKE GOOD WINE,
AND GROW STRONGER AS IT GROWS OLDER.**

—Old English Toast

DATE:

OCCASION:

LOCATION:

WINE NAME:

PRODUCER:

GRAPE VARIETIES:

VINTAGE:

REGION:

**SUB REGION OR SINGLE VINEYARD
(WHERE APPROPRIATE):**

OTHER NOTABLE BOTTLE INFORMATION:

APPEARANCE:

AROMA:

TASTE:

OVERALL IMPRESSIONS:

🍃 ____ UNIMPRESSIVE

🍃 🍃 ____ GOOD FOR EVERYDAY

🍃 🍃 🍃 ____ SPECIAL OCCASION

 WITH EACH GLASS OF THIS WINE, I DOUBLE
THE NUMBER OF FRIENDS I HAVE IN THIS ROOM.

DATE:

OCCASION:

LOCATION:

WINE NAME:

PRODUCER:

GRAPE VARIETIES:

VINTAGE:

REGION:

SUB REGION OR SINGLE VINEYARD
(WHERE APPROPRIATE):

OTHER NOTABLE BOTTLE INFORMATION:

APPEARANCE:

AROMA:

TASTE:

OVERALL IMPRESSIONS:

🍃 ____ UNIMPRESSIVE

🍃 🍃 ____ GOOD FOR EVERYDAY

🍃 🍃 🍃 ____ SPECIAL OCCASION

 **HERE'S TO THE TRIPLE ALLIANCE—
FRIENDSHIP, FREEDOM, AND WINE.**

DATE:

OCCASION:

LOCATION:

WINE NAME:

PRODUCER:

GRAPE VARIETIES:

VINTAGE:

REGION:

**SUB REGION OR SINGLE VINEYARD
(WHERE APPROPRIATE):**

OTHER NOTABLE BOTTLE INFORMATION:

APPEARANCE:

AROMA:

TASTE:

OVERALL IMPRESSIONS:

_____ UNIMPRESSIVE

_____ GOOD FOR EVERYDAY

_____ SPECIAL OCCASION

🍂 MAY OUR WINE BRIGHTEN THE RAYS OF
FRIENDSHIP, BUT NEVER DIMINISH ITS LUSTER.

DATE:

OCCASION:

LOCATION:

WINE NAME:

PRODUCER:

GRAPE VARIETIES:

VINTAGE:

REGION:

SUB REGION OR SINGLE VINEYARD
(WHERE APPROPRIATE):

OTHER NOTABLE BOTTLE INFORMATION:

APPEARANCE:

AROMA:

TASTE:

OVERALL IMPRESSIONS:

____ UNIMPRESSIVE

____ GOOD FOR EVERYDAY

____ SPECIAL OCCASION

🍃 HERE'S TO THE HEART THAT FILLS
AS THE WINE BOTTLE EMPTIES.

DATE:

OCCASION:

LOCATION:

WINE NAME:

PRODUCER:

GRAPE VARIETIES:

VINTAGE:

REGION:

SUB REGION OR SINGLE VINEYARD
(WHERE APPROPRIATE):

OTHER NOTABLE BOTTLE INFORMATION:

APPEARANCE:

AROMA:

TASTE:

OVERALL IMPRESSIONS:

🍃 ____ UNIMPRESSIVE

🍃 🍃 ____ GOOD FOR EVERYDAY

🍃 🍃 🍃 ____ SPECIAL OCCASION

 MAY WE NEVER WANT FOR WINE,
NOR FOR A FRIEND TO HELP DRINK IT.

DATE:

OCCASION:

LOCATION:

WINE NAME:

PRODUCER:

GRAPE VARIETIES:

VINTAGE:

REGION:

**SUB REGION OR SINGLE VINEYARD
(WHERE APPROPRIATE):**

OTHER NOTABLE BOTTLE INFORMATION:

APPEARANCE:

AROMA:

TASTE:

OVERALL IMPRESSIONS:

🍂 ____ UNIMPRESSIVE

🍂 🍂 ____ GOOD FOR EVERYDAY

🍂 🍂 🍂 ____ SPECIAL OCCASION

🍇 To you, and yours, and theirs, and mine,
I pledge with you, their health in wine.

DATE:

OCCASION:

LOCATION:

WINE NAME:

PRODUCER:

GRAPE VARIETIES:

VINTAGE:

REGION:

SUB REGION OR SINGLE VINEYARD
(WHERE APPROPRIATE):

OTHER NOTABLE BOTTLE INFORMATION:

APPEARANCE:

AROMA:

TASTE:

OVERALL IMPRESSIONS:

____ UNIMPRESSIVE

____ GOOD FOR EVERYDAY

____ SPECIAL OCCASION

🍇 HERE'S TO OUR NEXT JOYOUS MEETING—
AND, OH, WHEN WE MEET, MAY OUR WINE BE AS
BRIGHT AND OUR UNION AS SWEET.

DATE:

OCCASION:

LOCATION:

WINE NAME:

PRODUCER:

GRAPE VARIETIES:

VINTAGE:

REGION:

SUB REGION OR SINGLE VINEYARD
(WHERE APPROPRIATE):

OTHER NOTABLE BOTTLE INFORMATION:

APPEARANCE:

AROMA:

TASTE:

OVERALL IMPRESSIONS:

🍃 ____ UNIMPRESSIVE

🍃🍃 ____ GOOD FOR EVERYDAY

🍃🍃🍃 ____ SPECIAL OCCASION

🍇 MAY OUR WINE BRIGHTEN THE MIND
AND STRENGTHEN THE RESOLUTION.

DATE:

OCCASION:

LOCATION:

WINE NAME:

PRODUCER:

GRAPE VARIETIES:

VINTAGE:

REGION:

SUB REGION OR SINGLE VINEYARD
(WHERE APPROPRIATE):

OTHER NOTABLE BOTTLE INFORMATION:

APPEARANCE:

AROMA:

TASTE:

OVERALL IMPRESSIONS:

____ UNIMPRESSIVE

____ GOOD FOR EVERYDAY

____ SPECIAL OCCASION

🍃 **TO WINE: IT IMPROVES WITH AGE—I LIKE IT MORE THE OLDER I GET.**

DATE:

OCCASION:

LOCATION:

WINE NAME:

PRODUCER:

GRAPE VARIETIES:

VINTAGE:

REGION:

SUB REGION OR SINGLE VINEYARD
(WHERE APPROPRIATE):

OTHER NOTABLE BOTTLE INFORMATION:

APPEARANCE:

AROMA:

TASTE:

OVERALL IMPRESSIONS:

____ UNIMPRESSIVE

____ GOOD FOR EVERYDAY

____ SPECIAL OCCASION

A BOTTLE OF WINE CONTAINS MORE PHILOSOPHY THAN ALL THE BOOKS IN THE WORLD.—Louis Pasteur

DATE:

OCCASION:

LOCATION:

WINE NAME:

PRODUCER:

GRAPE VARIETIES:

VINTAGE:

REGION:

SUB REGION OR SINGLE VINEYARD
(WHERE APPROPRIATE):

OTHER NOTABLE BOTTLE INFORMATION:

APPEARANCE:

AROMA:

TASTE:

OVERALL IMPRESSIONS:

🍃 _____ UNIMPRESSIVE

🍃 🍃 _____ GOOD FOR EVERYDAY

🍃 🍃 🍃 _____ SPECIAL OCCASION

🍃 TO CHAMPAGNE, THE DRINK THAT MAKES YOU SEE DOUBLE, AND FEEL SINGLE!

DATE:

OCCASION:

LOCATION:

WINE NAME:

PRODUCER:

GRAPE VARIETIES:

VINTAGE:

REGION:

SUB REGION OR SINGLE VINEYARD
(WHERE APPROPRIATE):

OTHER NOTABLE BOTTLE INFORMATION:

APPEARANCE:

AROMA:

TASTE:

OVERALL IMPRESSIONS:

_____ UNIMPRESSIVE

_____ GOOD FOR EVERYDAY

_____ SPECIAL OCCASION

🍂 **WHEN I READ ABOUT THE EVILS OF DRINKING, I GAVE UP READING.**—Henny Youngman

DATE:

OCCASION:

LOCATION:

WINE NAME:

PRODUCER:

GRAPE VARIETIES:

VINTAGE:

REGION:

SUB REGION OR SINGLE VINEYARD (WHERE APPROPRIATE):

OTHER NOTABLE BOTTLE INFORMATION:

APPEARANCE:

AROMA:

TASTE:

OVERALL IMPRESSIONS:

🍂 ____ UNIMPRESSIVE

🍂 🍂 ____ GOOD FOR EVERYDAY

🍂 🍂 🍂 ____ SPECIAL OCCASION

🍇 **LET US HAVE WINE AND WOMEN, MIRTH AND LAUGHTER, SERMONS AND SODA WATER THE DAY AFTER.**—Lord Byron

DATE:

OCCASION:

LOCATION:

WINE NAME:

PRODUCER:

GRAPE VARIETIES:

VINTAGE:

REGION:

SUB REGION OR SINGLE VINEYARD (WHERE APPROPRIATE):

OTHER NOTABLE BOTTLE INFORMATION:

APPEARANCE:

AROMA:

TASTE:

OVERALL IMPRESSIONS:

_____ UNIMPRESSIVE

_____ GOOD FOR EVERYDAY

_____ SPECIAL OCCASION

🍂 ONE BOTTLE FOR FOUR OF US!
THANK GOD THERE'S NO MORE OF US!

DATE:

OCCASION:

LOCATION:

WINE NAME:

PRODUCER:

GRAPE VARIETIES:

VINTAGE:

REGION:

SUB REGION OR SINGLE VINEYARD
(WHERE APPROPRIATE):

OTHER NOTABLE BOTTLE INFORMATION:

APPEARANCE:

AROMA:

TASTE:

OVERALL IMPRESSIONS:

___ UNIMPRESSIVE

___ GOOD FOR EVERYDAY

___ SPECIAL OCCASION

TOO MUCH WORK, AND NO VACATION,
DESERVES AT LEAST A SMALL LIBATION.
SO HAIL! MY FRIENDS, AND RAISE YOUR GLASSES;
WORK'S THE CURSE OF THE DRINKING CLASSES.

DATE:

OCCASION:

LOCATION:

WINE NAME:

PRODUCER:

GRAPE VARIETIES:

VINTAGE:

REGION:

SUB REGION OR SINGLE VINEYARD
(WHERE APPROPRIATE):

OTHER NOTABLE BOTTLE INFORMATION:

APPEARANCE:

AROMA:

TASTE:

OVERALL IMPRESSIONS:

🍂 ____ UNIMPRESSIVE

🍂 🍂 ____ GOOD FOR EVERYDAY

🍂 🍂 🍂 ____ SPECIAL OCCASION

DRINK! FOR YOU KNOW NOT WHENCE YOU COME, NOR WHY; DRINK! FOR YOU KNOW NOT WHY YOU GO, NOR WHERE.—Omar Khayyam

DATE:

OCCASION:

LOCATION:

WINE NAME:

PRODUCER:

GRAPE VARIETIES:

VINTAGE:

REGION:

SUB REGION OR SINGLE VINEYARD
(WHERE APPROPRIATE):

OTHER NOTABLE BOTTLE INFORMATION:

APPEARANCE:

AROMA:

TASTE:

OVERALL IMPRESSIONS:

_____ UNIMPRESSIVE

_____ GOOD FOR EVERYDAY

_____ SPECIAL OCCASION

DRINK AND BE MERRY, FOR OUR TIME ON EARTH IS SHORT, AND DEATH LASTS FOREVER.—Amphis

DATE:

OCCASION:

LOCATION:

WINE NAME:

PRODUCER:

GRAPE VARIETIES:

VINTAGE:

REGION:

SUB REGION OR SINGLE VINEYARD
(WHERE APPROPRIATE):

OTHER NOTABLE BOTTLE INFORMATION:

APPEARANCE:

AROMA:

TASTE:

OVERALL IMPRESSIONS:

____ UNIMPRESSIVE

____ GOOD FOR EVERYDAY

____ SPECIAL OCCASION

HERE'S TO CHAMPAGNE, THE DRINK DIVINE,
THAT MAKES US FORGET OUR TROUBLES;
IT'S MADE OF A DOLLAR'S WORTH OF WINE
AND FOUR DOLLARS WORTH OF BUBBLES.

DATE:

OCCASION:

LOCATION:

WINE NAME:

PRODUCER:

GRAPE VARIETIES:

VINTAGE:

REGION:

SUB REGION OR SINGLE VINEYARD
(WHERE APPROPRIATE):

OTHER NOTABLE BOTTLE INFORMATION:

APPEARANCE:

AROMA:

TASTE:

OVERALL IMPRESSIONS:

🍂 ____ UNIMPRESSIVE

🍂 🍂 ____ GOOD FOR EVERYDAY

🍂 🍂 🍂 ____ SPECIAL OCCASION

🍇 THREE BE THE THINGS I SHALL NEVER ATTAIN: ENVY, CONTENT AND SUFFICIENT CHAMPAGNE. —Dorothy Parker

DATE:

OCCASION:

LOCATION:

WINE NAME:

PRODUCER:

GRAPE VARIETIES:

VINTAGE:

REGION:

SUB REGION OR SINGLE VINEYARD
(WHERE APPROPRIATE):

OTHER NOTABLE BOTTLE INFORMATION:

APPEARANCE:

AROMA:

TASTE:

OVERALL IMPRESSIONS:

____ UNIMPRESSIVE

____ GOOD FOR EVERYDAY

____ SPECIAL OCCASION

YOU ONLY HAVE SO MANY BOTTLES IN YOUR LIFE, NEVER DRINK A BAD ONE.—Len Evans

DATE:

OCCASION:

LOCATION:

WINE NAME:

PRODUCER:

GRAPE VARIETIES:

VINTAGE:

REGION:

SUB REGION OR SINGLE VINEYARD
(WHERE APPROPRIATE):

OTHER NOTABLE BOTTLE INFORMATION:

APPEARANCE:

AROMA:

TASTE:

OVERALL IMPRESSIONS:

____ UNIMPRESSIVE

____ GOOD FOR EVERYDAY

____ SPECIAL OCCASION

ALANSO OF ARAGON WAS WONT TO SAY IN COMMENDATION OF AGE, THAT "AGE APPEARS TO BE BEST IN FOUR THINGS—OLD WOOD BEST TO BURN, OLD WINE TO DRINK, OLD FRIENDS TO TRUST, AND OLD AUTHORS TO READ."—Francis Bacon

DATE:

OCCASION:

LOCATION:

WINE NAME:

PRODUCER:

GRAPE VARIETIES:

VINTAGE:

REGION:

SUB REGION OR SINGLE VINEYARD
(WHERE APPROPRIATE):

OTHER NOTABLE BOTTLE INFORMATION:

APPEARANCE:

AROMA:

TASTE:

OVERALL IMPRESSIONS:

_____ UNIMPRESSIVE

_____ GOOD FOR EVERYDAY

_____ SPECIAL OCCASION

🍇 **ONE NOT ONLY DRINKS WINE, ONE SMELLS IT, OBSERVES IT, TASTES IT, SIPS IT AND——ONE TALKS ABOUT IT.**—King Edward VII

DATE:

OCCASION:

LOCATION:

WINE NAME:

PRODUCER:

GRAPE VARIETIES:

VINTAGE:

REGION:

SUB REGION OR SINGLE VINEYARD (WHERE APPROPRIATE):

OTHER NOTABLE BOTTLE INFORMATION:

APPEARANCE:

AROMA:

TASTE:

OVERALL IMPRESSIONS:

____ UNIMPRESSIVE

____ GOOD FOR EVERYDAY

____ SPECIAL OCCASION

THERE'S LIFE AND STRENGTH ON EVERY DROP—THANKS-GIVING TO THE VINE!

—Albert Gorton Greene, *Baron's Last Banquet*

DATE:

OCCASION:

LOCATION:

WINE NAME:

PRODUCER:

GRAPE VARIETIES:

VINTAGE:

REGION:

SUB REGION OR SINGLE VINEYARD
(WHERE APPROPRIATE):

OTHER NOTABLE BOTTLE INFORMATION:

APPEARANCE:

AROMA:

TASTE:

OVERALL IMPRESSIONS:

____ UNIMPRESSIVE

____ GOOD FOR EVERYDAY

____ SPECIAL OCCASION

CHAMPAGNE WITH FOAMING WHIRLS AS WHITE AS CLEOPATRA'S MELTED PEARLS. —Lord Byron

DATE:

OCCASION:

LOCATION:

WINE NAME:

PRODUCER:

GRAPE VARIETIES:

VINTAGE:

REGION:

SUB REGION OR SINGLE VINEYARD
(WHERE APPROPRIATE):

OTHER NOTABLE BOTTLE INFORMATION:

APPEARANCE:

AROMA:

TASTE:

OVERALL IMPRESSIONS:

_____ UNIMPRESSIVE

_____ GOOD FOR EVERYDAY

_____ SPECIAL OCCASION

THE DISCOVERY OF A WINE IS OF GREATER MOMENT THAN THE DISCOVERY OF A CONSTELLATION. THE UNIVERSE IS TOO FULL OF STARS.—Benjamin Franklin

DATE:

OCCASION:

LOCATION:

WINE NAME:

PRODUCER:

GRAPE VARIETIES:

VINTAGE:

REGION:

SUB REGION OR SINGLE VINEYARD
(WHERE APPROPRIATE):

OTHER NOTABLE BOTTLE INFORMATION:

APPEARANCE:

AROMA:

TASTE:

OVERALL IMPRESSIONS:

____ UNIMPRESSIVE

____ GOOD FOR EVERYDAY

____ SPECIAL OCCASION

 BRONZE IS THE MIRROR OF FORM;
WINE, OF THE HEART. —Greek proverb

DATE:

OCCASION:

LOCATION:

WINE NAME:

PRODUCER:

GRAPE VARIETIES:

VINTAGE:

REGION:

SUB REGION OR SINGLE VINEYARD
(WHERE APPROPRIATE):

OTHER NOTABLE BOTTLE INFORMATION:

APPEARANCE:

AROMA:

TASTE:

OVERALL IMPRESSIONS:

____ UNIMPRESSIVE

____ GOOD FOR EVERYDAY

____ SPECIAL OCCASION

🍇 SINCE IN THIS SPHERE WE HAVE NO ABIDING PLACE, TO BE WITHOUT WINE AND A LOVER IS A MISTAKE.—Omar Khayyam

DATE:

OCCASION:

LOCATION:

WINE NAME:

PRODUCER:

GRAPE VARIETIES:

VINTAGE:

REGION:

SUB REGION OR SINGLE VINEYARD
(WHERE APPROPRIATE):

OTHER NOTABLE BOTTLE INFORMATION:

APPEARANCE:

AROMA:

TASTE:

OVERALL IMPRESSIONS:

🍃 ____ UNIMPRESSIVE

🍃 🍃 ____ GOOD FOR EVERYDAY

🍃 🍃 🍃 ____ SPECIAL OCCASION

 WINE HATH DROWNED MORE MEN
THAN THE SEA. —Thomas Fuller

DATE:

OCCASION:

LOCATION:

WINE NAME:

PRODUCER:

GRAPE VARIETIES:

VINTAGE:

REGION:

SUB REGION OR SINGLE VINEYARD
(WHERE APPROPRIATE):

OTHER NOTABLE BOTTLE INFORMATION:

APPEARANCE:

AROMA:

TASTE:

OVERALL IMPRESSIONS:

____ UNIMPRESSIVE

____ GOOD FOR EVERYDAY

____ SPECIAL OCCASION

WHERE THERE IS NO WINE THERE IS NO LOVE. —Greek proverb

DATE:

OCCASION:

LOCATION:

WINE NAME:

PRODUCER:

GRAPE VARIETIES:

VINTAGE:

REGION:

SUB REGION OR SINGLE VINEYARD
(WHERE APPROPRIATE):

OTHER NOTABLE BOTTLE INFORMATION:

APPEARANCE:

AROMA:

TASTE:

OVERALL IMPRESSIONS:

🍃 ____ UNIMPRESSIVE

🍃 🍃 ____ GOOD FOR EVERYDAY

🍃 🍃 🍃 ____ SPECIAL OCCASION

THE WINE URGES ME ON, THE BEWITCHING WINE, WHICH SETS EVEN A WISE MAN TO SINGING AND TO LAUGHING AND ROUSES HIM UP TO DANCE AND BRINGS FORTH WORDS WHICH WERE BETTER UNSPOKEN.—Homer, *The Odyssey*

DATE:

OCCASION:

LOCATION:

WINE NAME:

PRODUCER:

GRAPE VARIETIES:

VINTAGE:

REGION:

SUB REGION OR SINGLE VINEYARD (WHERE APPROPRIATE):

OTHER NOTABLE BOTTLE INFORMATION:

APPEARANCE:

AROMA:

TASTE:

OVERALL IMPRESSIONS:

_____ UNIMPRESSIVE

_____ GOOD FOR EVERYDAY

_____ SPECIAL OCCASION

WINE IS THE INTELLECTUAL PART
OF THE MEAL. —Alexander Dumas

DATE:

OCCASION:

LOCATION:

WINE NAME:

PRODUCER:

GRAPE VARIETIES:

VINTAGE:

REGION:

SUB REGION OR SINGLE VINEYARD
(WHERE APPROPRIATE):

OTHER NOTABLE BOTTLE INFORMATION:

APPEARANCE:

AROMA:

TASTE:

OVERALL IMPRESSIONS:

🍃 ____ UNIMPRESSIVE

🍃 🍃 ____ GOOD FOR EVERYDAY

🍃 🍃 🍃 ____ SPECIAL OCCASION

🍇 **WINE IS LIKE MUSIC—YOU MAY NOT KNOW WHAT IS GOOD, BUT YOU KNOW WHAT YOU LIKE!**

—Justin Meyer, American Winemaker

DATE:

OCCASION:

LOCATION:

WINE NAME:

PRODUCER:

GRAPE VARIETIES:

VINTAGE:

REGION:

SUB REGION OR SINGLE VINEYARD (WHERE APPROPRIATE):

OTHER NOTABLE BOTTLE INFORMATION:

APPEARANCE:

AROMA:

TASTE:

OVERALL IMPRESSIONS:

🍁 ____ UNIMPRESSIVE

🍁 🍁 ____ GOOD FOR EVERYDAY

🍁 🍁 🍁 ____ SPECIAL OCCASION

GOOD WINE RUINS THE PURSE;
BAD WINE RUINS THE STOMACH. —Spanish proverb

DATE:

OCCASION:

LOCATION:

WINE NAME:

PRODUCER:

GRAPE VARIETIES:

VINTAGE:

REGION:

SUB REGION OR SINGLE VINEYARD
(WHERE APPROPRIATE):

OTHER NOTABLE BOTTLE INFORMATION:

APPEARANCE:

AROMA:

TASTE:

OVERALL IMPRESSIONS:

____ UNIMPRESSIVE

____ GOOD FOR EVERYDAY

____ SPECIAL OCCASION

WINE MAKES EVERY MEAL AN OCASSION, EVERY TABLE MORE ELEGANT, EVERY DAY MORE CIVILIZED.—Andre Simon

DATE:

OCCASION:

LOCATION:

WINE NAME:

PRODUCER:

GRAPE VARIETIES:

VINTAGE:

REGION:

SUB REGION OR SINGLE VINEYARD
(WHERE APPROPRIATE):

OTHER NOTABLE BOTTLE INFORMATION:

APPEARANCE:

AROMA:

TASTE:

OVERALL IMPRESSIONS:

____ UNIMPRESSIVE

____ GOOD FOR EVERYDAY

____ SPECIAL OCCASION

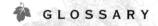 **GLOSSARY**

APPELLATION: The district where the grapes were grown.

BALANCED: In harmony, with the fruit, acid, tannin and alcohol working together to produce a seamless impression.

BACKWARD: A wine that seems younger than it is and will need more time to develop to maturity and reach its ideal state.

BODY: Neutral term for the overall texture and weight of a wine in the mouth, from light to big.

BOUQUET: The overall smell of a wine, particularly in relation to a wine with some age that is developing mature aromas.

CORKED: Used to describe a wine that has been tainted by a bad cork, making it smell like wet, moldy newspapers. Renders it unfit for tasting or drinking.

CLOSED: Not revealing many aromas and tastes on the nose or the palate.

Cloying: Describes a wine that is too sweet and therefore unbalanced.

Dry: Not giving the impression of sugar or fruit, usually meaning crisp or acidic, too.

Dumb: A wine that is going through a phase of being closed, which usually passes in a later stage of its aging development.

Earthy: Describes an aroma that evokes mushrooms, woods and soil. A good thing unless it becomes over the top and dirty.

Fat: Used to describe a wine that lacks acid and seems unstructured on the palate.

Finish: The last, lingering impressions of a wine. The longer the finish, the better.

Forward: Generally means the wine is immediately fruity and somewhere near its peak of development, not a candidate for aging.

Fresh: Having a lively acidity, usually describing a younger white.

Fruity: As distinct from sweet, having the pure, clean flavor of ripe fruits. This positive descriptor is common for younger wines.

Hot: Describes a wine with a discernibly high amount of alcohol. Generally speaking, table wines will have between 10 and 16 percent alcohol, which is always listed on the label.

Lean: Lacking in fruit, austere.

LEGS: The long drips that run down the side of a wine glass after the wine has been swirled. Full-bodied wines tend to have thicker, longer legs.

NOSE: The initial smell of a wine.

OAKY: A vanilla flavor that comes from aging in oak barrels.

OXIDIZED: A wine that has been in contact with air too long, making it lose fresh flavors and giving it a Sherry-like taste.

RESERVE: This word on a label usually means it has been specially treated, as in aged longer in wood; in countries like Spain ("reserva"), it has a legal definition.

STRUCTURE: Refers to the architecture of a wine, the way the acid, tannins and other textural elements combine to form a frame for the aromas and tastes.

TANNIN: The substance that coats your teeth in a red wine, giving it structure, texture and age-ability. It comes from grape skins and stems, as well as oak barrels.

TERROIR: A French word that literally means "soil" but has come to refer to the total characteristics of a particular vineyard—soil, weather, altitude and more—that can influence grapes. Saying that you can taste a wine's terroir is usually a compliment.

VARIETAL: The grape type. Chardonnay is an example of a varietal. Some wines are 100 percent of one varietal, but many are blends.

VEGETAL: Usually pejorative way to talk about wine that tastes like unripe vegetables, as distinct from the frequently positive note "herbal."